D1479240

THE TAO
THE SACRED WAY

Edited by
Tolbert McCarroll

STARCROSS BOOKS
Annapolis, California

*With appreciation
to the many people in many places
who have stumbled along the path of The Tao
throughout the years and given it life for this age.*

The Tao: The Sacred Way
1982 Version/Copyright © 1982 by Tolbert McCarroll
2018 Version/Copyright © 2018 by Tolbert McCarroll

"Path Photographs" Copyright © 2018 by Barbara Johannes

Second edition

Queries about information and permissions should be addressed to Starcross Books, 34500 Annapolis Rd., Annapolis, CA 95412. sj@starcross.org. (707) 886-1919. (www.starcross.org)

Design by Form & Content (www.formcon.com)
Printed in the United States of America

Cataloging-in-Publication Data
McCarroll, Tolbert (1931-)
    The Tao: The Sacred Way (attributed to Lao Tzu)
    1982 Version: ISBN 0-8245-0460-7
    2018 version: ISBN 978-0-9827329-4-6

    1. Spiritual. 2. The Tao. 3. Multi-Faith.

Library of Congress Control Number: 2017917537

BOOKS BY TOLBERT McCARROLL

Stepping Stones: Daily Reflections by an Unconventional Monk (2016)

Seasons: Through the Year with a Contemporary Monastic Family (2010)

A Winter Walk: Transcendent Moments when the Trees are Bare (2006)

Thinking with the Heart: A Monk and Parent Explores His Spiritual Heritage (2001)

Childsong/Monksong: A Spiritual Journey in the AIDS Pandemic (1994)

Morning Glory Babies: Children Living with AIDS and the Celebration of Life (1988, 1989, 1990)

A Way of the Cross: An Ancient Path in Ordinary Life (1985)

Guiding God's Children: A Foundation for Spiritual Growth in the Home (1983)

The Tao: The Sacred Way (Edited) (1982, 2018)

Notes from the Song of Life (1977, 1987, 2011): A Spiritual Companion

Exploring the Inner World: A Guidebook for Growth and Renewal (1974, 1976)

SOME WORDS OF BEGINNING...

The Tao has been an almost daily spiritual companion since I discovered a dusty copy in my Law School library in 1952. I edited a version, *The Tao: The Sacred Way,* that was published in 1982. As one reader recently put it, *"This book is the one that was around the house when I was a kid, and though I have enjoyed many versions since, and find that some have more clarity, this is the one that ties my decades together most completely. And that is the essence of the Tao; no right, no wrong interpretation. Just be."* He is right — just be. There have been a fairly large number of requests for the book to be available again. So here it is — refreshed. The philosopher Chuang Tzu (370–287 B.C.E.) wrote that wise people must guide themselves with the torch of chaos and doubt. That is certainly true of *The Tao!*

Who wrote *The Tao?* Long ago, some Chinese followers of *The Tao* put onto bamboo strips the learnings of their life. Here I call these people the "Old Ones." Perhaps there was a wise one called "Lao Tzu' who made this collection and tied the strips together. No one knows. The result is usually referred to as *The Tao* (path or way) *Te* (virtue) *Ching* (sacred book). It is said that there are almost as many editions of *The Tao* as of the *Bible* and *Bhagavad Gita*. Naturally, some similar phrases will appear in various editions.

All of the many versions of *The Tao* are different and all are the same. None are accurate and none are false. Ancient Chinese writing was not limited by the desire for preciseness. It more resembled a series of pictures. The people who would learn the message must swim in the characters and in the spaces around them. What is not written is equal in importance to what is written. Nothing can be seen by examining a page of the book, unless at the same moment we examine our hearts and our experiences.

All the many versions of *The Tao* now available are indications of a wide-spread turning to Eastern spiritual wisdom. The Cistercian monk and student of Asian spirituality, Thomas Merton (1915–1968), expressed it this way on his first, and unfortunately fatal, trip to Asia: *"I am going home, to a home where I have never been."* He spoke for many of us.

It seems to me that editions of *The Tao* fall roughly into two categories: (1) scholarly works, especially after the discovery of the ancient Ma-wang-tui texts; and (2) works produced to help people, of all faiths or none, on their spiritual path. I think of these as "backpack editions." I have often recommended the versions of Gia-Fu Feng (1919–1985) which, combined with the photography of his wife, Jane English, have become something of a classic in making the wisdom of the *Tao Te Ching* more accessible. In recent years, there have been many versions of *The Tao* published. I have found that in every new version that has come into my hands there has been something fresh which expanded my understanding of the book I have lived with for so many years. I am particularly impressed by the versions produced by people who are traveling on some particular spiritual path in their own lives; Tibetan or Zen

Buddhism, Judeo-Christian approaches, Native Americans, Sufi, Yoga, non-theistic, atheistic, etc., etc. To me, this gives proof that the *Tao Te Ching* is a living document that will go on being changed and being applied long into the future.

However, Pema Chödrön, who grew up in an American Catholic family and is now a Buddhist nun and director of Gampo Abbey, gives us all a serious warning. She uses the first line of the *Tao Te Ching,* which is, as Gia-Fu Feng and others translate it, *"The Tao that can be told is not the eternal Tao."* That, writes Pema Chödrön, is perhaps the most important line in the book. I would agree. She would like to see it translated, *"As soon as you begin to believe in something, then you can no longer see anything else."* Pema Chödrön continues, *"The truth you believe in and claim to makes you unavailable to hear anything new."* I have tried to keep this caution in mind as I worked my way through my own version.

It is fascinating to me that words originally meant to counsel Chinese rulers in governing their states centuries ago have evolved into guiding untold numbers of present day spiritual seekers in living their daily lives.

A major influence on my version of *The Tao* was an ongoing seminar I was privileged to facilitate in 1973–1974. It was part of a program to find bridges between Humanistic Psychology and the spirituality of both East and West. Thirty people of differing backgrounds, lifestyles, and occupations met weekly in San Francisco. Each week, we focused on a particular chapter of *The Tao* and shared experiences of how it applied to and influenced our lives. Many versions of *The Tao* were in use. I asked participants to use two or more versions which they selected themselves. I generally used three: an anonymous British text, a translation by Arthur Waley (1889–1966) published in 1958 and later accepted in a cultural series of UNESCO, and also one translated by John C.H.Wu (1899–1986), a close friend of Thomas Merton.

Like Merton, I make no claim to being a student of Chinese languages, either modern or ancient. I know only a few characters. I have relied on old texts and when necessary the valuable contribution of friends. And again, as Merton said in his *The Way of Chuang Tzu, "I do not think that this book calls for blame; if someone wants to be unpleasant about it he can blame me and my friends."* In my case, the number of friends was rather large, each with at least two versions of *The Tao!*

On mornings after each meeting, using my notes from the session, I tried to pull things together and find a contemporary application of the chapter emerging from the discussions. It was not a straight-forward process. As the Venerable Abbot Chao Khun Saana Sobhana has said about spiritual growth in general and the reading of old texts, *"One must ascend all the steps, but then, when there are no more steps, one most make the leap."* Making that leap beyond the words is both the frightening challenge and the wonderful adventure of the spiritual life.

For me, those weekly seminars encouraged "the leap." They helped make *The Tao* a living spiritual way and also resulted in the publication of *The Tao: The Sacred Way.* Such gatherings are still going on at various places. I am told that one in New England is called "Beer and Tao!" I was very moved in a recent workshop when a 22-year-old related something stimulated by *The Tao* that was a completely new concept for me! And it was very poignant to be with another person who had lived with *The Tao* all her life and through her final illness. On her peaceful journey to the other shore, she was, I am sure, floating in the waters of *The Tao.*

Is *The Tao* prose or poetry? This version, and a number of others, came along in California while the influence of the San Francisco Renaissance in Poetry could still be felt. At the time of that movement, Ezra Pound (1885–1972) had found and completed Ernest Fenollosa's (1853–1908) work on *The Chinese Written Character as a Medium for Poetry.* Poet friends attempted to explain it to me. They failed! All I remember that is relevant here is: there are few incidental words in Chinese such as "is". Nouns (and indeed all words) have a verbal undertone. As a result, there is action in all words, as well as in the empty spaces; every action is close to nature; and there is no real grammar. One friend looked at my blank stare in frustration and said, *"Just like poetry, read it as poetry!"*

There are three terms that appear often in this book.

 ***The Tao* (pronounced something like "Dow").** Half of the character starts with some hair joined to a head. That made "head." The other half has three parts in it: to step with the left foot and to halt and to walk step by step. From these comes a feeling of wholeness; head and foot, round and square, stop and go. *Tao* is not a phenomenon or a being. Some medieval Christian mystics distinguished between "God" and the "Godhead." Perhaps *The Tao* and the Godhead are the same concept. By its very nature, *The Tao* in unfathomable, yet it can

be relied upon. Once you have given up your ideas of what *The Tao* is, turn to chapter 25 and read a description of it.

Te (pronounced something like "**Deh****"). This means "Virtue" or the moral force and strength that comes from living a consistent and whole life. The character is made of three parts: "to go"/"straight"/"to the heart." It is not a prissy virtue, but like the Latin word *vir* from which "virtue" stems, *Te* reflects a strength. *Te* is the manifestation of *The Tao* that is produced through the instrument of people, animals, plants, and all things that are completely committed to being themselves. There is nothing mysterious about acquiring Virtue. If you eat well, you are not undernourished. If you exercise, you get strong. If you follow *The Tao,* you obtain Virtue.

Shung Ren. This is usually translated as "Sage" or "Wise Person." Looking at the history of the phrase, I feel it means *"a person who has a duty to listen."* I have searched for a lot of words to express this and for a while used the word "Saint." In Western languages, it meant a holy person. The word "holy" intertwined in Old English with concepts of wholeness and health. But there are too many connotations to "Saint," so I settled on a parallel concept used by the ancient followers of *The Tao* and usually translated "True Person." This book is written for those who wish to heed the call to completeness by becoming more courageous and compassionate themselves, learning to be more at home on the earth and living in such a way as to add some pure and still moments to the rhythm of life. I have told this is close to the Buddhist concept of "Bodhisattva."

I divided this work into two books. This follows an ancient practice. The first book was sometimes called *"Classic of Tao"* and the second was given the name *"Classic of Te."* There is a difference and a sameness about the two books — like breathing in and breathing out.

The Tao is universal. It is not Chinese. Its essence is found in the spiritual quest of every culture and age on earth. Before this story began and after it ends, there is *The Tao*. It consists of stillness and silence. It will enter into any quiet heart.

There are no footnotes or commentary here. These words of *The Tao* are to be hung like bells in our hearts and rung by the motions we make as we move through our daily lives. Any other sounds make it difficult to hear the bells.

I live at Starcross Monastic Community. Many of our friends have found this book of value in their lives. This is not just a book in our library but one that rests in our chapel, on our work benches, by our beds, in our backpacks and pockets. We often open it and try to live with it. As we have done this over the years we have come to realize that we hold a flower that will never stop unfolding. May this flower grow well in your garden.

Tolbert McCarroll
Sonoma County, California

HERE BEGIN
THE SAYINGS OF
THE OLD ONES

THE
FIRST
BOOK

道德聖人

· 1 ·

The Tao that can be spoken is not the ultimate Tao.
The names that can be used are not the true names.

The beginning of heaven and earth is without name.
What can be named are the many things encountered.

Send your desires away and you will see the wonders of life.
Be filled with desire and you will see only the reflections.
These spring up in different ways but share the same root.

Deep darkness surrounds
      the gateway to the great and sacred emptiness.

·2·

When something is labeled beautiful
    the sense of ugliness is created.
When it is common to consider something good
    other things are denounced as bad.

Therefore something and nothing give birth to one another.

The same is true of:
    easy and difficult,
    long and short,
    high and low.
Yet different notes can harmonize with one another.
The beginning and the end can relate to one another.

Nourish them without claiming authority.
Benefit them without demanding gratitude.
Do the work, then move on.

And, the fruits of your labor will last forever.

·3·

Not praising the talented prevents rivalry.
Not valuing goods that are hard to obtain presents stealing.
Not displaying desirable things prevents discontent.

Therefore, the True Person helps others by:
    calming their minds,
    feeding them well,
    discouraging antagonism,
    and keeping their bodies strong.
If the people are simple and free from desire,
    then the clever ones never dare to interfere.

Practice action without striving
    and all will be in order.

·4·

The Tao is like an empty bowl,
    yet it can be used
    without ever needing to be filled.
It is the deep source
    of the ten thousand things.

Dull the edge.
Untie the knot.
Soften the brightness.
Settle with the dust.

It is concealed yet present.
I do not know whose child it is.
It is older than the common ancestor.

·5·

Heaven and earth are not moved
        by offerings of straw-dogs.
The True Person is not moved
        by offerings of straw-dogs.

The space between heaven and earth is like a bellows.
It is empty and yet never exhausted.
The more it works the more comes out.

Many words lead to exhaustion.
Better to hold fast to your center.

·6·

The valley spirit never fails.
It is the unknown first mother,
	whose gate is the root
	from which grew heaven and earth.
It is dimly seen, yet always present.
Draw from it all you wish;
	it will never run dry.

· 7 ·

Heaven and earth are enduring.
The reason why heaven and earth endure
    is that they do not live for themselves.
Hence, they endure.

Therefore, the True Person
    leaves self behind
    and thus is found in front,
    is not guarded and thus is preserved,
    is self-free and thus is able
    to find fulfillment.

·8·

The highest form of goodness is like water.
For water benefits the ten thousand things without effort.
It settles in places that people avoid
　　and so is like The Tao.

In choosing your home look to the land.
In preparing your heart go deep.
In associating with others value gentleness.
In speaking exhibit good faith.
In governing provide good order.
In the conduct of business be competent.
In action be timely.

When there is no strife, nothing goes amiss.

.9.

Keep on pouring and it will overflow.
Keep on grinding and destroy the blade.
Bring gold and jade into the house,
    and no one can protect it.
Be prideful about wealth and position,
    and disaster will follow.
Stop when the work is finished —
This is the path to a peaceful life.

·10·

While carrying your active life on your head
      can you embrace the quiet spirit in your arms,
      and not let go?
While being fully focused on your vital breath
      can you make it soft like that of a newborn babe?
While cleaning your inner mirror
      can you leave it without blemish?
While loving the people and guiding them
      can you dispense with cleverness?
While opening and closing the gates of heaven
      can you be like a mother bird?
While questing after insight
      can you remain simple?

Help the people live!
Nourish the people!

Help them live yet lay no claim to them.
Benefit them yet seek no gratitude.
Guide them yet do not control them.
This is the hidden Virtue.

·11·

Thirty spokes connect to the wheel's hub;
     yet it is the center hole
     that is of benefit.
Clay is shaped into a vessel;
     yet it is the emptiness it surrounds
     that is of benefit.
Walls are put up for a house
     yet it is the space within
     that is of benefit.

We labor for what is there
     but we benefit from what is not.

·12·

Colors can blind the eye.

Notes can deafen the ear.

Flavors can spoil the taste.

Racing and hunting drive the mind wild.

Goods that are hard to obtain hinder the journey.

Therefore, the True Person
  trusts inner wisdom
  and thinking with the heart.

·13·

Both favor and disgrace bring fear.
Great trouble comes from having a body.

What is meant by:
    "Both favor and disgrace bring fear?"
Favor leads to a fear of losing it and
    disgrace leads to a fear of greater trouble.

What is meant by:
    "Great trouble comes from having a body?"
The reason we have trouble is that
    we are self-conscious.
No trouble can befall a self-free person.

Therefore, let us surrender our self-interest,
and love others as much as we love ourselves
Then we can be trusted to care for all things.

·14·

Look at it, you cannot see it.
It is invisible.
Listen to it, you cannot hear it.
It is inaudible.
Reach for it, you cannot grasp it.
It is intangible.

These three qualities are unfathomable
   and so they fuse together and become one.

The upper part is not bright.
The lower part is not dark.
Ceaselessly it moves back to nothingness.
It has the form of the formless,
        the image of the imageless.
It is indefinable and shadowy.
Go up to it and we will not see its front.
Follow it and we will not see its back.

Yet, hold fast to the ancient way
        and experience the present now-moment.
Know the beginnings and
        we can follow the path.

·15·

The ancient followers of The Tao
  were subtle, inscrutable and shrewd.
They were often too deep to be understood.
We can only describe their appearance.
Hesitant, as if crossing a frozen river.
Watchful, as if aware of neighbors on all sides.
Respectful, like a visiting guest.
Fluid, like ice beginning to melt.
Blank, like an uncharted block.
Open, like a valley.
Obscure, like muddy water.

Who else can be still and let the muddy water
        slowly become clear?
Who else can remain at rest and slowly come to life?

Those who hold fast to The Tao
        do not try to fill themselves to the brim.
Because when they do not try to be full
        they can be worn out and yet ever new.

·16·

Empty everything out;
     hold fast to your stillness.
Even though all things are stirring together,
     watch for the movement of return.
The ten thousand things flourish and then
     each returns to the root from which it came.
Returning to the root is stillness.
Through stillness each fulfills its destiny.
That which fulfills its destiny
     becomes part of the Always-so.
To be aware of the Always-so is to awaken.

Those who innovate while in ignorance of the Always-so
move toward disaster.
Those who act with awareness of the Always-so
embrace all, are not possessed by particular desire
and move toward The Tao.
Those who are at one with The Tao abide forever.
Even after their bodies waste away,
they are safe and whole.

·17·

The best leader is one whose existence
    is barely known by the people.
Next comes one whom they love and praise.
Next comes one they fear.
Next comes one they defy.

Leaders who do not trust enough will not be trusted.

True Persons do not offer words lightly.
When their task is accomplished
    and their work is completed,
        the people say, "It happened to us naturally."

·18·

When the great Tao is forgotten,
    benevolence and moral codes arise.
When shrewdness and cleverness appear,
    great hypocrisy follows.
When there is no harmony in the family,
    filial manners are developed.
When the country is in disorder,
    ministers appear as loyal servants.

·19·

Stop being learned and your troubles will end.

Give up wisdom, discard cleverness,
and the people will benefit a hundredfold.

Give up benevolence, discard moral judgments,
and the people will rediscover natural compassion.

Give up shrewdness, discard gain,
and thieves and robbers will disappear.

These three false adornments are not enough to live by.
They must give way to something more solid.
Look for what is natural and hold onto the uncarved block.
Diminish thoughts of self and restrain desires.
Avoid vainglorious learning. Value simplicity.

·20·

Give up being correct and be yourself.

What is the difference between "good" and "not good?"

Must I like what others like? How silly!

Everyone else is enjoying a great celebration.
I am not and don't care.
I am drifting without direction,
    like a baby who has not yet smiled.

While everyone else has more than they need,
    I feel in want.
My mind is empty. I am confused.
Other people are alert and self-assured,
    I alone feel dull and muddled.
I am as unsettled as the waves of the sea.
It seems as if everyone else has a purpose,
    but I drift awkwardly.

I am different from other people,
Even so, I am nourished by the great mother.

·21·

The Great Virtue is to follow The Tao.

The Tao can be obscure.
Faint and evasive, yet within it is a form.
Within it is a substance.
Within it is a vital force,
    which is real and can be relied upon.

From ancient times to the present, The Tao's instructions
    have not been forgotten.
Through it can be perceived the beginning of the story
    of life.
How do I know how it was at the beginning of the story
    of life?
Because of what is within me.

·22·

Give way and be unharmed.
Soften and find strength.
Empty out and be content.
Grow old and be renewed.
Have little and be secure.
Have much and be confused.

Therefore, the True Person embraces the source
    and becomes a model for all.

Do not look only at yourself
    and you will see much.
Do not justify yourself,
    and you will be respected.
Do not brag
    and you will have merit.
Do not be prideful
    and your work will endure.

It is because you do not strive
    that no one under heaven can strive with you.

The saying of the Old Ones, "Give way and be unharmed,"
    is not a meaningless phrase.
True wholeness is achieved
    by blending with life.

·23·

To follow nature use only simple and quiet words.
A whirlwind does not last all morning,

    and a sudden shower does not last all day.
Who produces these things? Heaven and earth!
If even heaven and earth cannot make wild things last long
How can people hope to do so?

People of The Tao
	conform to The Tao.
People of virtue
	conform to virtue.
People who lose the way
	conform to the loss.
Those who conform to The Tao
	become part of The Tao.
Those who conform to virtue
	are welcomed into virtue.
Those who conform to the loss
	are welcomed into the loss.

Those without convictions
	do not inspire confidence.

·24·

The person on tiptoe does not stand firm.
The person who races ahead does not go far.

Those who look only at themselves see little.
Those who justify themselves are not respected.
Those who brag have no merit.
The work of prideful people will not endure.

From the standpoint of The Tao,
    these things are like tumors.
As they bring sickness,
    followers of The Tao steer clear of them.

·25·

Something undefined yet complete,
    existing before heaven and earth.
Silent and limitless,
    it stands alone and without change.
Yet reaching everywhere, it does not tire.
Perhaps it is the mother of all things on earth.
I do not know its name
    but I call it "Tao."

When I have to describe it I call it "great."
Being great it keeps going.
It goes far away.
Going far away, it comes back.

Therefore, The Tao is great.

Heaven is great.

Earth is great.

People are also great.

Thus, people constitute one of the
    four great things of the universe.

People conform to the earth.

The earth conforms to heaven.

Heaven conforms to The Tao.

The Tao conforms to its own nature.

·26·

Solidness is the root of lightness.
Stillness controls restlessness.

Therefore, wise people when traveling all day
    do not lose sight of their baggage cart.
Although there are beautiful sights to see,
    they remain quietly in their place.

Should the owner of thousands of carts
    appear more frivolous than a simple traveler?

To be light is to lose the root.
To be restless is to lose self-control.

·27·

Walk well and leave no trail.
Speak well and cause no dispute.
Calculate well and there is no error.
A well made door needs no bolt
        yet it cannot be opened.
A well made fastening requires no knot
        yet it cannot be untied.

Therefore, the True Person is skillful in assisting people,
        and abandons nobody;
Is skillful in taking care of things,
        and abandons nothing.
This is called "being guided by the inner light."

Therefore, the skillful person is the teacher
        of the person without skill.
The person without skill is the material
        for the skillful person.

If you do not respect the teacher,
    if you do not care for the student,
    you are on the road to confusion
    and your cleverness will not save you.

This is an essential principle of The Tao.

·28·

Develop masculine strength
    but live by feminine gentleness.
Become a brook and receive all things under heaven.
If you are such a brook
    then virtue will constantly flow into you
    and you will return to the simplicity of a child.

Know the pure
    but live the life of the sullied.
    Become a fountain for all things under heaven.
If you become such a fountain
    then you will have abundant virtue
    and you will return to the state of the uncarved block.

When the uncarved block is cut up into pieces,
    it is tuned into useful vessels.
But the True Person makes use of it whole.

Hence, it is said, "The finest carver cuts little."

·29·

Whoever wishes to take over the world
will not succeed.

The world is sacred
and nothing should be done to it.
Whoever tries to tamper with it
will mar it.
Whoever tries to grab it
will lose it.

Hence, there is a time to go ahead
        and a time to stay behind.
There is a time to breathe easy
        and a time to breathe hard.
There is a time to be vigorous
        and a time to be gentle.
There is a time to gather
        and a time to release.

Therefore, the True Person avoids extremes,
        self-indulgence, and extravagance.

·30·

If you would assist leaders of people
    by way of The Tao,
you will oppose the use of armed force to overpower
    the world.

Those who use weapons will be harmed by them.
Where troops have camped only thorn bushes grow.
Bad harvests follow in the wake of a great army.

The skillful person may have to strike a blow but must then stop,
    without taking advantage of victory.
Bring it to a conclusion but do not be vain.
Bring it to a conclusion but do not be boastful.
Bring it to a conclusion but do not be arrogant.
Bring it to a conclusion but only when there is no choice.
Bring it to a conclusion but without violence.

When force is used, youthful strength decays.
This is not the way of Tao.
And that which goes against The Tao
    will quickly pass away.

·31·

Weapons are ill-omened things.

Among gentle people the left side
    is the place of honor when at home,
    but in war the right side is the place of honor.

Weapons are not proper instruments for gentle people;
    they use them only when they have no other choice.
Peace and quiet are what they value.
They do not glory in victory.
To glorify war is to delight in the slaughter of people.
Those who delight in the slaughter of people will
    never thrive among all that dwell under heaven.

The army that has killed people
    should be received with sorrow.
Conquerors should be received with the rites of mourning.

·32·

The Tao is eternal yet nameless.

Although the uncarved block is small,
    it is not inferior to anything under heaven.
When people keep hold of the block
    everything works together.
Heaven and earth unite and sweet dew falls.
The people live in harmony
    without any law or decree.

Only when the block is carved
    do different names appear.
As soon as there are names
    it is time to stop.

Know when to stop and avoid danger.
Let all under heaven return to The Tao
    as brooks and streams flow home to the sea.

·33·

To know others is to be clever.

To know yourself is to be wise.

To overcome others requires forcefulness.

To overcome yourself requires strength.

To know that you have enough is to be rich.

Push through and you may get your way,

    but return home and you will endure.

Live out your days and you have had a long life.

·34·

The great Tao covers everything like a flood.
It flows to the left and to the right.
All things depend on it
    and it denies none of them.
It accomplishes its task yet claims no reward.
It clothes and feeds all things
    yet it does not attempt to control them.
Therefore, it may be called lowly.

The ten thousand things return home to The Tao
    even though it does not control them.
Therefore, it may be called great.

So it is that the True Person does not wish to be great
    and therefore becomes truly great.

·35·

Hold The Tao in your thoughts
    and all under heaven will come to you without fear.
Coming to you and not being harmed,
    they will find rest, peace and security.

A passing guest will pause at the sound of music
    and the smell of fancy food.
By comparison The Tao is mild and flavorless.
It is not solid enough to be seen,
    nor loud enough to be heard.
Yet, it lasts forever.

·36·

That which is to be shrunk
    must first be stretched out.
That which is to be weakened
    must first be strengthened.
That which is to be overthrown
    must first be set up high.
That which is to be taken,
    must first be given.

There is wisdom in dimming your light.
For the soft and gentle
    will overcome the hard and powerful.

Fish are best left in deep waters.
And, weapons are best kept out of sight.

·37·

The Tao never strived,

    yet it completes everything.

If people adhere to it

    then all things will grow of their own accord.

If after they have developed

    they experience desires to strive,

    they can bury those desires

    under the simple uncarved block.

Simplicity can protect

    against desire.

When desires are restrained there will be peace,

    and then all under heaven will be at rest.

THE
SECOND
BOOK

·38·

A highly virtuous person is not conscious of virtue
    and therefore possesses virtue.
A person of little virtue tries to appear virtuous
    and therefore lacks virtue.
A highly virtuous person does not make a fuss.
A person of little virtue always makes a fuss.
A truly good person functions without ulterior motive.
A loyalist acts out of private desires.
A ritualist acts and, when no one responds,
    rolls up a sleeve and marches.

When we lose The Tao, we turn to virtue.
When we lose virtue, we turn to kindness.
When we lose kindness, we turn to the law.
When we lose legality, we turn to ritual.

Ritual is the mere husk of good faith and loyalty
    and the beginning of disorder.
Knowledge of what is to come
    may be a flower of The Tao,
    but it is the beginning of folly.

Hence, the well-formed person relies on what is solid
    and not on what is flimsy,
    on the fruit and not the flower.
Therefore, such a person lets go of that without
    and is content with this within.

·39·

From ancient times these things have arisen from the one:
> Heaven is clear because of the one,
> The earth is firm because of the one,
> The spirit is strong because of the one,
> The valley is full because of the one,
> The ten thousand things reproduce because of the one,
> People are able to lead because of the one.

All of this comes from the one.

If heaven were not clear it would soon split.
If the earth were not firm it would soon bend and break.
If the spirit were not strong it would soon wear out.
If the valley were not full it would soon dry up.
If the ten thousand things did not reproduce
> they would soon die out.
If people could not lead they would soon fall.

Therefore, greatness has its source in the little.
The low is the foundation of the high.

When people call themselves "alone," "helpless," "worthless,"
    is this not acknowledging a humble root?

Enumerate the parts of a horse
    and that is not a horse.
Better to resound like stone chimes
    than to tinkle like jade bells.

·40·

Returning is the direction of The Tao.
Yielding is the way of The Tao.

All things are born of something
　　and something is born of nothing.

·41·

The wise person on hearing The Tao
  diligently puts it into practice.
The average person on hearing The Tao
  keeps is one minute and loses it the next.
The shallow person on hearing The Tao
  laughs at it loudly.
If this person did not laugh it would not be The Tao.

Therefore, the ancient proverb says:

The way into light may seem dark.
The way forward may seem backward.
The even path may seem up and down.
The greatest whiteness may seem soiled.

Great virtue may seem like a canyon.
Abundant virtue may seem inadequate.
Vigorous virtue may seem limp.
Simple virtue may seem faded.

The greatest square has no corners.
The most useful vessel takes long to complete.
The softest note is hard to hear.
The greatest image has no shape.

The Tao is hidden and unnamed
yet it is The Tao alone that supports all things
and brings them to completion.

·42·

The Tao gives birth to the one.
One gives birth to two.
Two gives birth to three.
And three gives birth to the ten thousand things.

The ten thousand things have their backs in the shadow of
Yin, the still force,
    while they embrace the light of Yang, the active force.
Harmony is achieved by blending
    these two forces.

People dislike feeling alone, helpless, worthless,
    yet this is how wise people often describe themselves.

So it is that sometimes a thing is increased
    by being diminished and
    diminished by being increased.

I have learned this from history
    "A violent person will not often die a natural death."
It is well to remember this.

·43·

The most yielding of all things
    overcomes the hardest of all things.
That which has no substance
    can enter where there is no opening.

Hence, I know the value of action without action.

Few things under heaven bring more benefit than
    the lessons learned from silence and
    the actions taken without action.

·44·

Your reputation or your body:

    Which is more important?

Your body or your possessions:

    Which is worth more?

Gain or loss:

    Which is more painful?

Thus it is that the miser will pay much.

The hoarder will suffer great loss.

Be content with what you have

    and you will not be disgraced.

Know when to stop

    and you will not be harmed.

Only in this way will you be secure forever.

·45·

It is complete, but missing something,
    yet it keeps going.
It is full, but seems empty,
    yet it will never drain out.

The straight looks bent.
The skillful seems clumsy.
Powerful speech sounds like stammering.

Moving overcomes cold,
    stillness reduces heat.

The calm and quiet set right
    everything under heaven.

·46·

When The Tao prevails in the world
    horses help in the fields.
When The Tao is unheeded
    horses are trained for war on the border lands.

There is no greater offense than harboring desires.
There is no greater calamity than not knowing what is enough.
There is no greater sorrow than coveting more.

Hence, if you are content,
    you will always have enough.

·47·

Without stepping out your door,
   you can know everything under heaven.
Without looking out your window,
   you can know the way of heaven.
The farther you travel,
   the less you know.

Therefore, the True Person
   arrives without traveling,
   perceives without looking,
   and acts without striving.

·48·

In the pursuit of learning,
    every day something is added.
In the pursuit of The Tao,
    every day something is dropped.

Do less and less
    until you come to action without striving.
When you follow this practice,
    nothing remains undone.

Understanding all under heaven comes from
    letting things take their course.
No real knowledge can be gained by meddling.

·49·

The True Person does not have an individual heart
     but uses the heart of the people.

The True Person
     is kind to those who are kind,
     is also kind to those who are not kind.
Thus, there is an increase in kindness.

The True Person
     keeps faith with those who are in good faith,
     also keeps faith with those who lack good faith.
Thus, there is an increase of good faith.

The True Person is detached and humble
     and to the world appears peculiar.
Other people strain their eyes and ears,
     yet the True Person smiles like a child.

·50·

When going off one way means living
    and going off the other way means dying,
    three in ten are companions of Life,
    three in ten are companions of Death, and
    three in ten value Life but drift toward Death.

Why is all this so?
Because, these people are too greedy about living.

It is said:
    People who are skillful in caring
    for the life that has been given to them
    travel abroad without fear of wild ox or tiger,
    and enter a battle without concern for sharp weapons.
    There is no place for the wild ox to thrust its horns,
    there is no place for the tiger to put its claws,
    there is no place for a weapon to lodge.

How is this so?
Because, there is no place for Death to enter in!

·51·

The Tao gives life to all things,
  and its virtue nourishes them,
  forms each according to its nature
  and gives to each its inner strength.

Therefore, all things venerate The Tao
  and honor its virtue.
It has never been decreed that The Tao be venerated
  and its virtue be honored;
  they have always been so treated spontaneously.

Thus, The Tao gives life to all things;
        and its virtue raises them, nourishes them,
        brings them to their full growth,
        feeds, shelters, and protects them.

Giving life without possessing,
        benefiting without expecting gratitude,
        guiding without control.
This is called the hidden virtue.

·52·

All things under heaven had a common beginning,
    and that beginning could be considered
    the mother of all things.
When you know the mother
    you will also know the children.
Know the children, yet hold fast to the mother,
    and to the end of your days
    you will be free from danger.

Block the passages!
Shut the doors!
And, to the end of your days
    your strength will not fail you.
Open the passages!
Increase your activities!
And, to the end of your days
    you will be beyond help.

See the small and develop awareness.

Practice yielding and develop strength.

Use the outer light but return to the inner light
and save yourself from harm.

This is known as following the Always-so.

·53·

If I have the least bit of awareness,
     I will walk upon the great path of Tao
     and only fear straying from it.
This great way is straight and smooth
     yet people often prefer the side roads.

The courtyard is well kept
     but the fields are full of weeds,
     and the granaries stand empty.
Still, there are those of us
     who wear elegant clothes, carry fancy swords,
     pamper themselves with food and drink
     and are overflowing with wealth.
These are the actions of thieves.

This is certainly far from The Tao.

·54·

What is well rooted cannot be pulled up.
What is tightly embraced will not be lost.
It will be forever held in honor.

When cultivated in your person, virtue will be real.
When cultivated in your household, virtue will be plentiful.
When cultivated in your village, virtue will abound.
When cultivated in your world, virtue will become widespread.

Hence, through yourself look at Self.
Through your household look at Household.
Through your community look at Community.
Through your country look at Country.
Through your world look at World.

How do I know that the world is like this?
Because of what is within me.

·55·

A person who is filled with virtue
    is like an infant.
Poisonous insects will not sting,
    wild animals will not attack,
    birds of prey will not swoop down.
Although bones are soft and sinews weak,
    a child's grip is firm.
The union of man and woman is not known,
    yet there is completeness,
    because a child's vital force is at its height.
Crying all day will not produce hoarseness,
    because there is perfect harmony.

To know harmony is to know the Always-so.
To know the Always-so is to be awakened.

Trying to fill life to the brim invites a curse.
For the mind to make demands upon the breath of life
    brings strain.

Whatever has been forced to a peak of vigor
    approaches its decay.
This is not the way of The Tao.
And that which goes against The Tao
    will quickly pass away.

·56·

The person who knows does not speak.
The person who speaks does not know.

Block the passages!
Close the doors!
Blunt the sharpness!
Untangle the knots!
Soften the glare!
Settle with the dust!
This is the mystery of evenness.

Those who have achieved this cannot be enclosed
    nor kept at a distance;
    they cannot be benefited nor harmed,
    honored nor disgraced.

Therefore, this is the noblest state under heaven.

·57·

Govern the country by being straightforward.
Being crafty is for waging war.
Win all under heaven by not meddling.

How do I know that this is so?
By what is within me.

The more rules there are,
    the more impoverished the people.
The more pointed the people's weapons,
    the more disorder there is in the country.
The more crafty the people,
    the stranger their lives become.
The more laws and edicts that are posted,
    the more outlaws that arise.

Hence, an Old One has said:

    I act without striving and the
        people transform themselves.
    I love stillness and the
        people straighten themselves.
    I do not meddle and the
        people prosper by themselves.
    I am free from desires and the
        people themselves return to the simplicity
        of the uncarved block.

·58·

When the government is unseen
　　　the people are simple and happy.
When the government is oppressive
　　　the people are crafty and discontented.

On misery perches happiness.
Beneath happiness crouches misery.

Who knows when this will cease?
The straight changes into the crooked.
The good becomes the ominous.
Surely the people have been confused for a long time.

Therefore, the True Person squares without cutting,
　　　carves without slashing,
　　　straightens without dislocating,
　　　gives forth light without blinding.

·59·

In guiding others it is best to use moderation.

A person who is moderate returns to the path.

Returning to the path brings an abundance of virtue.

This good store of virtue cannot be conquered.

Virtue that cannot be conquered knows no limit.

Only a person who has limitless virtue is fit to lead.

Only a person who cares for the people

    as a mother cares for her child

        will long endure.

This is called making the roots go deep

    by restraining the trunk.

Learn to focus your life and you will see many days.

·60·

Governing a big country is like frying a small fish.

Let all under heaven be governed in accordance with The Tao,
    and evil forces will not manifest their power.
It is not that they lack power
    but rather they will not use their power
    to harm the people.
They are not the only ones who have power
    and do not use it to harm the people.
The True Person does not harm the people.
Whenever there is no harm done,
    that power flows into the common virtue.

·61·

A great country is like the low ground
  where all the streams unite.

In all things under heaven
  the female overcomes the male by her stillness,
  and because she is still she lies below.

Hence, if the great country will take the low place
  it will win over the little country.
If the little country will take the low place
  it will win over the great country.

Thus, the one gets below and prospers
  and the other remains below and prospers.
All that the great country wants is more people.
All that the little country wants is a place
  for its people to go and be employed.
If each is to get what it needs
  it is necessary for the great country
  to take the low place.

·62·

The Tao is to the ten thousand things
  what the shrine is in the home.
It is the treasure of the virtuous
  and the protection of the wrongdoer.

Good words are appreciated.
Good deeds are accepted as gifts.

Even the wrongdoers are not abandoned.

Hence, on the day a monarch is installed
    and appoints important ministers,
    remain where you are and make an offering of The Tao.
It will be preferable to a gift of jade discs
    followed by a team of four horses.
Why did the ancients value The Tao?
Was it not because through it
    you can find what you seek,
    and because of it
    you can escape what is hounding you?

Therefore, it is the most valuable thing under heaven.

·63·

Act without striving.
Work without interfering.
Find the flavor in what is flavorless.

Enlarge the small, increase the few.
Heal injury with goodness.

Handle the difficult while it is still easy.
Cultivate the great while it is still small.

All difficult things begin as easy things.
All great things begin as small things.

Therefore, the True Person never attempts anything great,
and accomplishes great things.

Lightly made promises inspire little faith.
Trying to make things easy results in great difficulties.

Therefore, the True Person regards everything as difficult,
and is never overcome by difficulties.

·64·

Peace is preserved while things are still at rest.
Trouble is averted before it starts.
What is fragile is easily broken.
What is small is easily lost.

Handle a problem before it appears.
Secure order before a crisis begins.

A tree as big as a person's embrace begins as a tiny seedling.
A terrace nine stories high rises from a shovelful of dirt.
A journey of a thousand miles begins with the first step.

A person who interferes does harm,
    and one who clutches loses hold.
Therefore, the True Person acts without striving and
    does no harm,
    avoids clutching and never loses hold.

People often ruin their ventures
        when they are nearly complete.
So, tend as carefully to the end as to the beginning
        and your work will not be ruined.

Therefore, the True Person tries to be free from desire,
        does not value things that are hard to come by,
        learns without scholarship,
        leads people back to what they have passed by,
        and helps the ten thousand things return to their true natures,
        all without daring to interfere.

·65·

The ancients who practiced The Tao
    did not use it to enlighten the people,
    but rather to assist them in gaining simplicity.
The reason people are difficult to govern
    is because they try to be clever.

Hence, a person who attempts
    to govern a country by cleverness
    will injure it.
Those who govern without cleverness
    will benefit the country.
These are the two models.
Knowing these models is called the mystic virtue.
The mystic virtue is deep and so far-reaching
    that it can lead all things back
    toward great harmony.

·66·

How does the sea control a hundred streams?
By taking the lower place the sea
    controls a hundred streams.

Therefore, when True Persons are over the people
    they speak humbly.
When they lead the people
    they stand behind the people.

When True Persons are given a place above the people
    they do not crush the people with their weight.
When they take their place ahead of the people
    they do not obstruct the people's progress.
That is why everything under heaven supports them gladly
    and does not tire of them.

Because they strive with no one,
    no one can strive with them.

·67·

All people respect me
        but think what I say is strange
        and resembles nothing else.
It is because The Tao is great that it is unlike anything else.
If it were like anything on earth
        it would have been small from the beginning.

I have three treasures that I cherish.
        The first is compassion,
        the second is simplicity,
        the third is not striving to be first
                among all things under heaven.
Because of compassion I am able to be brave.
Because of simplicity I am able to be generous.
Because of not striving to be first
        I am able to lead.

If people forsake compassion and attempt to be brave,
     forsake simplicity and attempt to be generous,
     forsake the last place and attempt to get to the first place,
     this will surely lead to death.
Compassion overcomes in conflict and defends when under attack.
What heaven nourishes, it arms with the gift of compassion.

·68·

A skilled warrior does not rush ahead of others.
A skilled fighter does not make a show of anger.
A skilled victor does not seek revenge.
A skilled employer does not act superior.

This is known as the virtue of not competing.
This is known as making use of the talents of others.
This is known as harmonizing with heaven
    as in ancient times.

·69·

The master soldiers have a saying:
 rather than be the host I prefer to be the guest,
 rather than advance an inch
  I prefer to retreat a foot.

This is called marching without taking steps,
 rolling up a sleeve without baring an arm,
 seizing a foe without a battlefront,
 arming yourself without weapons.

There is no disaster greater than attacking
 and finding no enemy.
Doing so will cost you your treasure.
Thus it is that when opposing forces meet,
 victory will go to those
 who take no delight in the situation.

·70·

Although my words are easy to understand
    and easy to practice,
    no one understands them
    or puts them into practice.

My words have an ancestor. My actions are governed.

People do not understand this,
    hence, they do not understand me.
Those who understand me are few.
Those who follow me should be respected.

Therefore, the True Person wears homespun clothes
    and carries jade in the heart.

·71·

It is well to know that you do not know.
To think you know when you do not is sickness.

When you are sick of sickness you will be well.
True Persons are well because they are sick of sickness;
    this is the way to health.

·72·

When the people no longer respect you
    disaster will descend.

Do not constrict their living space.
Do not oppress them in their work.
If you do not oppress them, they will not grow tired of you.

Therefore, True Persons know themselves
    and do not make a show of themselves.
They know their value
    but do not act exalted.
They prefer this within to that without.

·73·

A person whose courage lies in daring will meet death.
A person whose courage lies in not daring
    will encounter life.
Of the two courses, one is beneficial
    and the other harmful.

Heaven dislikes what it dislikes.
Who knows the reason why?
Even the True Person has difficulty with such a question.

The Tao of heaven
    does not strive and yet it wins,
    does not speak and yet it gets responses,
    does not beckon and yet it attracts,
    is at ease and yet it follows a plan.

Heaven's net covers all.
Though the mesh is coarse, nothing escapes.

·74·

When the people do not fear death,
     of what use is it to threaten them with death?
If the people were always afraid of death
     and if those who did wrong
     would always be arrested and put to death,
     who would do wrong?

There is always an executioner
     whose duty it is to kill.
If you try to fill that function
     it is like trying to hew wood
     in place of a master carpenter.
You will probably injure your own hands.

·75·

Why do the people go hungry?

Because their leaders devour too much of the tax-grain;

that is why the people go hungry.

Why are the people difficult to govern?

Because their leaders stand in their way;

that is why the people are difficult to govern.

Why do the people treat death lightly?

Because their leaders are so grossly absorbed

in the pursuit of living;

that is why the people treat death lightly.

Indeed, it is wiser to ignore life altogether

than to place too high a value on it.

·76·

People are born supple and soft.
At death they are rigid and hard.
Grass and trees are pliant and tender when living,
    but they are dry and brittle when dead.
Therefore, the stiff and hard are attendants of death,
    the supple and soft are attendants of life.

The person who relies only on strength will face defeat.
The rigid tree will break in the wind.

Therefore, the hard and mighty are vulnerable;
    the yielding and gentle are secure.

·77·

The way of heaven is like stringing a bow.
The high end is pulled down and the low end is raised up.
The excessive is diminished
and the deficient is supplemented.

It is the way of heaven to take where there is surplus
in order to give where there is scarcity.
The way of people is otherwise.
They take from those without
in order to benefit those with too much.
Who will take from their own excesses
and give to all under heaven?
Only those who hold to The Tao.

Therefore, the True Person benefits yet expects no reward,
does the work and moves on.
There is no desire to be considered better than others.

·78·

Nothing under heaven is
     more supple and yielding than water.
Yet there is nothing like it
     for breaking down the hard and stiff.

Everyone knows that the yielding overcomes the tough
     and the soft overcomes the hard.
Yet no one applies this knowledge.

Therefore, an Old One said:
     Only a person who has accepted the country's dirt
          is a leader worthy to offer sacrifice
          at its shrines of earth and grain.
     Only a person who takes up the country's burdens
          should lead.

The truth often seems false.

·79·

Even though a truce is made between great enemies,
  some enmity will linger.
How can this be beneficial?

Therefore, the True Person
  undertakes the obligations of the agreement
  but makes no claim upon others.
The person of virtue shares with others.
The person who lacks virtue takes from others.

The way of heaven has no favorites;
  it ever abides with good people.

·80·

Let countries be small with few people:
>   Though there may be machines that would increase
>   production ten to a hundred times
>   they are not used.
>   The people are mindful of death and do not
>   journey to far places.

They have ships and wagons but no one uses them.
They have a warehouse of weapons
>   but there is no occasion to display them.

The people give up writing
     and return to knotting cords.
They are satisfied with their food.
They are pleased with their clothes.
They are content with their homes.
They delight in their simple ways.

They can see another country
     and can hear dogs barking and cocks crowing in it,
     still the people grow old and die
     without ever coming into conflict.

·81·

Sincere words are not elegant;
    elegant words are not sincere.
The virtuous person does not dispute with others;
    the person who disputes is not virtuous.
The wise do not have great learning;
    those with great learning are not wise.

True Persons do not hoard.
Using all they have for others, they still have more.
Giving all they have to others, they are richer than before.

The way of heaven is to benefit and not to harm.
The way of the True Person is to assist without striving
    in the unfolding of the story of the earth.

HERE END
THE SAYINGS OF
THE OLD ONES

ACKNOWLEDGMENTS

There have been many helping hands in this venture. Foremost has been Sister Julie De Rossi, a talented publication associate, who rendered invaluable assistance as she worked beside me, line by line. She has lived with *The Tao* for many years and was in many ways a co-editor of this venture. Essential were the participants in the Wednesday Seminars, and Professor Hobart "Red" Thomas, and his colleagues in the Psychology Department of Sonoma State University and members of the Association of Humanistic Psychology who encouraged and helped guide the project. I make no claim to being a student of Chinese languages, either modern or ancient. I have relied on old texts and, when necessary, the valuable contribution of friends, especially Meiko Omi and her family, and Paul D. Clasper and his students. Paul was a professor at The Graduate School of Theology in Berkeley and also served as Dean of St. John's Cathedral in Hong Kong. This edition was greatly enhanced by the "Path Photographs" of my friend and neighbor Barbara

Johannes. Like everything else I have attempted, this has been made possible with the help of my many spiritual companions, and students of the Way of The Tao for over half a century. Thank you all! And so here it is — ready for more backpacks!

TOLBERT McCARROLL, *better known as "Brother Toby," has lived by Meister Eckhart's adage that what a person acquires by contemplation should be spent in compassion. Hans Küng (1928-), President of the Global Ethic Foundation, described him as a person of courage and creativity leading "to new forms of spiritual life and social involvement." Brother Toby established homes for children impacted by the AIDS pandemic in California, Romania, and Uganda and is a founding member of the multi-faith Starcross Monastic Community in the hills of Northern California. He is the author of 11 spiritual books, including the classic* Notes from the Song of Life *and, most recently,* Stepping Stones: Daily Reflections by an Unconventional Monk. *Now in his late 80s, Brother Toby is increasingly looking for God in nature and the ordinary moments of life. He takes great delight in his children, music, a cup of tea, and his cat, Tigger.*